In this comic ...

Superdog

Superman

Melanie

Kevin

Superdog went into space ...
... when he was just a pup!
But there was a problem.
Alert!
It became a long voyage!
Sleep gas began to seep into the space pod!

The pod flew to Earth.
I slept for ages!
I've grown up!
The pod gave Superdog a badge ...
Whoosh!

Superdog landed on Earth!
Honk!
Yikes! I'm in the way!
Honk!
I'll jump.
I'm flying!
Strange!

A city! I might find a friend there.
WELCOME TO MUDGE CITY
A boy was looking for a friend too.
Would you like to play frisbee?
I'll play!
Chluck!
Swush!
Ha ha ha!
Get that!

I've nearly got it ...
Ha ha ha!
Snap!
Help!
Whoosh!
I'm flying!

You fly like Superman ... and you have the 'S' badge!
This gadget will help you understand me.
Who are you?
I'm Kevin.
I'll call you Superdog!
Home time ...
Min's
I have no home.

Kevin took
Superdog home.
Superdog
was happy.
He seems nice.

Chomp!
A giant leap!
Superdog had lots of energy!

They made a kennel.
Superdog put his pod ...
... underground!

Later ...
Who drew this?
My owner, long ago.
Let's see the news!
LIVE
A ship is in danger ...
METRO
... it has zoo cargo!
Go, Superdog!

You need a
costume. Like it?
Just the cape
is okay!
It's a plane!
It's a bird!

It must be Superman!
Whoosh!
Strange ... it's a dog!
Yay!
Zing!
I'll fix the ship.
Whoosh!
Superdog!
Job sorted.

Look!
He must be Superman's dog!
Doggy is Superdog!
No, Melanie, he just looks the same!
Later ...
What do you smell?
Sniff!
Sniff!
Sniff!
My old owner.

It's Superman!
Ruff!
Ruff!
Superdog!
He belongs to you?
Yes, from long ago!
So you drew these?
Yes. Gee, he was just a pup!
Do you need him back?

I'm away a lot ...
Ruff!
... can he stay with you?
Yes!
Good dog.
I'll be back!

I'm so happy!
Ruff!
Ruff!
Go, Superdog!